Pulse

110 Principles, Ideas & Virtues for Women Living, Not Just Existing

by Sinita Wells

COPYRIGHT © 2022 BY SINITA WELLS

All rights reserved. No part of this book may be reproduced or transmitted in any form or by any means without the written permission from the author.

I DEDICATE this book to

ALL the beautiful women of the world dedicated to themselves, their growth and abundance. Without you believing and loving you first, nothing else is possible in your world. You deserve to be appreciated. Always continue to strive for your very best, letting everything else fall into place. **YOU ARE WORTH IT!**

Contents

INTRODUCTION

CH 1: THE GRAND IDEA — 7
The Essentials To Attaining Life's Success

CH 2: HAPPINESS — 13
The Best Things In Life Are Free

CH 3: SETTING GOALS — 23
Hitting The Mark

CH 4: ME TIME — 32
The Best Things In Life Are Free

CH 5: MONEY MATTERS — 39
Be Financially Stable

CH 6: LIFE IN GENERAL — 47
Basic Survival Tips

CH 7: RELATIONSHIPS — 52
How to Make Them Last

CH 8: SHIT HAPPENS — 63
How To Win With Everyday Agonies

CH 9: BEATING THE ODDS — 71
What To Do When Things Do Not Go As Expected

CH 10: BEATING THE ODDS — 77
When Broken Relationships Do Not Go As Expected

CH 11: GUILTY AS CHARGED — 83
When The Problem Is You

CH 12: REGAINING YOUR STRENGTH — 89
In Life, Love and Everything Else

CH 13: END OF THE ROAD — 98
Zoning In On What You Want

CH 14: TOP 8 VIRTUES — 104
To Enjoy a More Prosperous Life

INTRODUCTION

We all want to succeed in life. And though success is hard work, it is still what everybody wants. Therefore, people get up in the morning work their ass off, drag their tired bodies back to bed at night, just to do it all over again, day after day. People simply want better.

The key is to move the images we have in our heads to the reality we call life. So why not approach it realistically, logically and with clear understanding.

Pulse is dedicated to women who are ready to live this life. They are tired of just existing only to do the bare minimum of getting by in life. They want to escape the mundane and be free to be happy from the inside out.

Inside you will find **110 principles, tips and virtues** that you can use to improve your life and prosper at whatever you desire. There may be advice that you have already heard before, but it is said, repetition is the mother of all learning. So, check your pulse and let's dive in.

"Work Your Dreams Until They Become Your Reality, Then Dream Some More"

~Sinita Wells

CHAPTER 1
THE GRAND IDEA:

The Essentials To Attaining Life's Success

PRINCIPLES 1-6

1 Own The Proper Mindset

Whether you want to simply cross the street or build an empire, you must have it in you. Having the right attitude is always the first requirement to getting things done. The stories that have been told to you or that you have heard growing up does not make them true for your life. Create a mindset that works for you and what you want to become and present to the world. And, honestly it is the only credential that you will need. **Be your authentic you.**

2 Be mindful

Information is power and if you do not stick out your ear to whatever is happening, there simply would be no direction. You do not always have to know everything, but it would matter a lot if you know what matters. Be open and willing to always invest in your learning. We've all heard the saying, "A mind is a terrible thing to waste." Don't waste the brain that you have been granted. **Fill it up wisely.**

3 BE HEALTHY

Do not be naïve and think that you can have it made by intellect alone. Eat and drink the right amount of food and water, keeping yourself healthy is the major key to the stamina needed to build your empire. If you want to accomplish your goals you simply must be around to do so, right? So, get into a healthy routine to keep your body and mind moving. **Thirty minutes a day is all you really need.**

4 USE YOUR COMMON SENSE

It stings to hear or even read that statement, but it is true. Statistics have been piling on just how many people lose everything just because they don't use common sense. Everything is not book smarts. It can be that voice that tells you to go right, but you go left. It is that gut feeling that tells you option B is the better choice. It is hardwired in every individual and it actually makes things easier. **So, check in and trust yourself.**

5 Show Up

You do not get to be called a leader if you do not perform leader responsibilities and showing up is part of it. Whether you work in the real world or through the Internet, "showing up" shows your commitment to yourself, your family and those you are purposed to serve. **Would you follow you?**

6 Follow Through

When building any type of relationship, the best thing you can do is follow through on what you say you will do. It's always better to over deliver. **Relationships are what build success.**

My Thoughts

Date:

"When Nothing is Sure Everything is Possible"

~Margaret Drabble

CHAPTER 2
HAPPINESS:

Best Things In Life Are Free

PRINCIPLES 7-20

7 Appreciate The Little Things

Find a reason to be happy. It does not always have to be a person or something big. In fact, you would be astonished at how the little things can affect you in big ways. A smile, saying hello, the sunshine on your face, the beautiful sounds of nature or your significant other leaving out your favorite coffee cup in the morning. Big things are great, but little things are memorable. **Who was the last person you did a little something for?**

8 Smile

Smiling transcends almost all differences. It may feel like a silly gesture, but it is a formula that works and has been proven with time. And you never know how a simple smile can make someone's day. **Smile for no reason today and watch how others respond.**

9 Smell The Coffee

If you are a coffee drinker, like I am, the aroma alone can be enough to rev up your nerves and create a more beautiful day. If not, "smell the coffee" in whatever way relates to you. A hot cup of tea or a nice glass of wine (yes, it's always 5 o'clock somewhere) can create the same beautiful day. **What is your favorite "make my day" drink?**

10 Stretch Far Out While You Yawn

Stifling a yawn during a meeting is one thing, but rising up from bed and stretching like you mean it is another. Try extending your arms so far out that you can almost hear your muscles contract. That is your signal that you have been given another opportunity to be amazing. **Stretch like you mean it!**

11 SCREAM FOR ALL THE WORLD TO HEAR

Simply living the day to day of life can be challenging. Sometimes to draw positive energy, you must first release the bad energy. Relinquish the negativity by screaming at the top of your lungs, sure you will scare the neighbors, but it will sure feel good. Plus, it don't cost you a thing. **Ready? 1…2…3…GOOOOO!**

12 LET THEM FLOW

If screaming is not your thing, then try having a good cry. The best thing you can do for yourself is let it go. Whatever has put you in a funk needs to be released. It cannot stay bottled up inside. So, let them flow and move on. It always make me feel better. **When was the last time you had a good cry?**

13 HAVE SEX

Yes, I said it! Now, if screaming and crying does not do it for you, have mind-blowing sex (which in turn may make you scream and cry) with someone you love in places you have never done it before. It does not have to be all 50 shades of grayish (unless that's your thing), but one toe curling orgasmic experience will really make you happy. The oxytocin that the brain releases are sure to make you feel heavenly. **It's how you got here in the first place, right?**

14 SING TO YOUR FAVORITE TRACK

Humming is safe but singing aloud is more satisfying. Have you ever pulled up next to a car and they are just grooving to the music? It kind of makes you feel good too, right? If having an audience is not your thing, then close the blinds, pump up the volume and let the rhythm take control. **What is your favorite sing out loud song?**

15 WATCH THE STARS

Celebrities may be good-looking people but the big dipper, Venus and all the other twinkling stars are better to gaze at. In the country on my grandmother's farm, the stars are so clear and bright. Just take a moment or two to revel in the presence of a million stars and you would be happy to realize they might all be twinkling for you. **Can you find the big and little dipper?**

16 FINISH A BOOK

Turn off the television and read that book that you took time to order, pay for and is sitting on your nightstand right now. A chapter a night should get the job done. **What was the last book you've read?**

17 Have A Chat With A Toddler

Annoying aside, kids are the funniest creatures on earth. Not only can they make a big deal out of the simplest things, but they can do it in a way that does not irritate you like your significant other does. I know my gbabies have me fussing one minute, then laughing the next. **When was the last time you just talked to a little one?**

18 Converse With People

We live in a digital world now, but wouldn't it be nice to just sit and talk to other people, share your interests and listen to their stories. You can use the experience to learn new things, improve your own skill or dispel myths that you have grown to believe. The world is full of diverse ideas, backgrounds, beliefs and ways of life. Explore the experiences of others to expand your mind. **You never know what new things you will learn.**

19 Laugh Out Loud

People forget to laugh sometimes because the more engrossed with life people get, the lesser we find the humor in it, but the benefits of laughing are far too great that not finding a single reason to laugh is hilarious within itself. **LOL because YOLO!**

20 Pick Up the Phone

Again, in this digital world we are so connected, but so distant. Wouldn't it be nice to pick up the phone and dial a friends' number? Have a personal conversation with someone, especially if you have not talked in a while. Checking for them on social media is cool, but it cost nothing to pick up the phone. **"Hello, is it me you're looking for?"**

My Thoughts

Date:

"If, everyday, I dare to remember that I am here on loan, that this house, this hillside, these minutes are all leased to me, not given, I will never despair"

~Erica Jong

CHAPTER 3
SETTING GOALS:
Hitting The Mark

PRINCIPLES 21-31

21 Write Down Your Priorities

It would help you significantly to write your goals down instead of just thinking about them inside your head. Invest in a journal or a good notebook – it will keep you on track and will also serve as a reminder at how many milestones you have achieved so far. **When was the last time you journaled?**

22 Be Realistic

Setting realistic goals would bring you closer to success. You can achieve anything you believe, but start smart and set realistic goals that will lead up to the bigger ones. **What can you achieve in the next 90 days, realistically?**

23 Be Specific

Getting a promotion and getting a promotion within the year are two different goals. You must know which among your goals need to be accomplished within a certain amount of time. Procrastinating is the worst kind of company in goal setting. **What is the exact date to achieve the first goal?**

24 Build Your Tribe

Surround yourself with like-minded individuals who will believe in you, encourage you and support you. Never forget the people who helped you along the way. Thank them as you go along and then thank them again upon completing a goal. **Who do you need to thank?**

25 DELEGATE

You can't build an empire all alone. You may start out as the lone ranger, but as your dreams grow so will the need for help grows. Know when you need to call for help. Also know what lane you are great in then delegate where you are not so great. **It is okay to ask for assistance.**

26 ACCEPT CRITICISMS

…from the right people, those that love you and want the best for you. It hurts more when people criticize your work, but it is one facet of life that is inevitable. Rather than sulking, use the information to your advantage or better yet, prove to them that you are better and bigger than what they make of you. **Use their criticism as your fuel for learning and an opportunity to grow and do better.**

27 Engage In A Friendly Competition

As Darwin put it, the human race is built to outdo each other. Well, there is no sense putting a stop to it now, but make it friendly. A little friendly competition can be healthy. **Who is your friendly competition?** And don't say "Yourself". Who is someone that you follow, like or admire that you say, "I wouldn't mind living that type of life." Then strive for it. They don't even have to know.

28 Do It For Yourself

You will never satisfy everybody. So, don't try. Live **YOUR LIFE** for YOU. Do what you want to do how you want to do it. There will always be those that don't like it. Guess what? Their problem not yours. You will never be truly satisfied if you allow people or trends to dictate your life. You want to wear blue hair, go for it! **You only have one life to live, right?**

29 Prove Them Wrong

Everyone is not going to believe in you. Everyone will not want you to succeed. There will be people you look up to that will tell you what you can't or won't be. You don't have to do any explaining. Your greatest gift you can give yourself is to prove them wrong. **It's not their assignment. It's yours.**

30 Rejoice In Your Success

Sometimes, people forget to congratulate themselves even after accomplishing a goal. It is okay to pat yourself on the back. You have worked your ass off and deserve the recognition. **Look in the mirror, right now and say GOOD JOB!**

31 Finish Strong

Do not be in a rush to cross out all your hopes, dreams and wishes. It doesn't have to take forever either. But, accomplishing your goals one by one will help relieve overwhelm and frustration. I always say, take bite size chunks. Before you know it, your plate will be empty.

It's not how you start, it's how you finish. Remember the tortoise and the hare? **What is that FIRST goal you want to see come to pass?**

My Thoughts

Date:

"We are always afraid to start something that we want to make very good, true and serious"

~Brenda Ueland

CHAPTER 4
ME TIME:

Commit to Yourself

PRINCIPLES 32–39

32 Me, Me and Me

Take this pledge. Repeat after me. I am not being selfish. I love, give and support all those that I have been called to. But, today I commit to put ME FIRST. This is not a selfish act. It is a selfless act. In order to give my true and authentic love, I must understand the importance of loving ME FIRST. For those that cannot understand my position, I am okay with that. You have the right not to participate in how I am designing my life. No hard feelings. **Signed, I Am A Wo (Man) First.**

3.3 Write A Love Letter

We have all made choices we may not be proud of. If we knew better I am sure we would have done better. Forgiveness of self is the key. There should be no one that loves you more than you love you. Writing a love letter to yourself and **Set Yourself Free!**

34 ENJOY A BUBBLE BATH

No matter what age or sex you are, bubble baths can gratify the soul within. Light some candles and play soft music to complete the picture. Allow yourself to revel in the pleasures that never fail to amuse. **Ahhh, take me away!**

35 BE ALONE

Being alone and loneliness are two different things. Once you begin to love yourself enough you will never be lonely. In fact, you will begin to appreciate your own company. Establishing #metime for yourself is essential to self-love. It allows you to get to know you and appreciate the greatness that you are. **When was the last time you took yourself out on a date?**

36 Go Places

Whether it's alone or with friends, travel to places, experience different cultures, visit destinations and most of all, expand your reach. There is simply no use waiting to enjoy life. **Where was the last place you visited?**

37 Check Yourself Out

It's okay to love and appreciate what your mama gave you. Not in an arrogant kind of way, but a self-loving kind of way. It's not about how you look, but how you carry yourself from the inside out. Create a vibe that says you are a valuable asset in life and in business. **Love the skin you are in.**

38 Do What You've Been Putting Off

Procrastination is not your friend. Repeat after me, PROCRASTINATION IS NOT MY FIREND. You have been putting it off long enough. This is the year of YES. Yes to yourself, writing your book, starting your business, getting healthy. Yes, yes and yes! **No more excuses. PERIOD!**

39 Respect Yourself

You don't ever have to compromise who you are, your morals or your beliefs. The greatest gift of self-love is honesty and respect. When you look in the mirror and you are proud of the person looking back at you, you have hit the mark. **Walk with your head held high.**

My Thoughts

Date:

"When we live life centered around what others like, feel, and say, we lose touch with our own identity"

~Neva Coyle

CHAPTER 5
MONEY MATTERS:

Be Financially Stable

PRINCIPLES 40-48

40 Identify The Source Of Your Income

The first rule to becoming financially stable is to know where your money is coming from. This way, you will know when you will have money, how much is coming and so on. Knowing that it takes this amount to build your empire will help you save and stop spending on frivolous things. Keep track of the bottom line so that you can continue your success track of financial abundance. It takes money to make this life better. **What is your annual money goal?**

41 Set Up Multiple Bank Accounts

You must have separate bank accounts for emergency, savings and daily expenditures and business. Setting a limit to each will not only secure your future but curtail unnecessary spending too. You cannot and should not comingle your personal and business expenses. Be smart and do it right. **Do you have separate accounts set up?**

4.2 Do Not Spend More Than You Can Afford

We are all guilty of not making smart money choices. I sure am. When they approached you in college with those credit cards, we were like, YES!! You get a card, I get a card, we all get a card… LOL. They came to bite us in the ass later, right? Now that we are older and wiser, we can make different choices. Keep your credit cards for emergencies only. If you can't pay cash, you can't afford it. **Words to live by.**

4.3 Do Not Loan What You Can't Afford To Give

There is a reason why you must be cautious when lending your money – you may or may not get it back. It does not mean that you have to be greedy either, but it would really help to choose whom to help. If you can afford it then sure give it. If not, it is quite alright to say No. **You know NO, is a complete sentence, right?**

4.4 SAVING ALONE WILL NOT ADD TO YOUR MONEY

Venture into business, buy stocks or go into trading if you have to. There are a lot of ways that you can add value to what you already have. Sometimes it is not all about having money, but knowing how to generate an income out of it that makes it all worth your while. Diversify yourself. Create several streams of income. Like your mama said, "Do not put all your eggs in one basket." **You're liable to drop them. Then what?**

4.5 GET INSURED

The reason a lot of us go into business or work hard is to leave your family better off. So, be smart and get insured in many ways. For your business, your car, your home, your health, YOUR LIFE. The smallest things can set you back tremendously. It may seem like it will never happen to you, but it can come when least expected or ready. **What insurance coverage do you need to buy today?**

46 You Must Treat Money Differently

One of the secrets of wealthy people is that they use their money to grow more money. We must learn to tell ourselves a different story when it comes to money. Not all of us grew up learning the value of money. A lot of us probably heard negative things about money. Like, money don't grow on trees. Technically it does i.e., paper...LOL. How about, money is the root to all evil? Well, hell I better stay away from it. We need to learn that it's okay to have money. It's okay to build wealth. And it's okay to enjoy the finer things that money can bring to our lives as long as we have it in our hearts to serve and give back. To whom much is given, much is required. **Money is a tool.**

47 BE CHEAP

You would be surprised how frugal the rich can be. So, when you find yourself with more money, do not be a big spender. Learn the art of bargaining as it is not because you don't have it, but you want to get the best for your hard-earned dollar. **Money don't grow on trees *wink*.**

48 BE HUMBLE

To whom much is given, much can be taken away. Never forget where you came from. Always be grateful for the grace you have been granted. As quick as you rise is a quick as you can fall if you put your energy in the wrong vibrations. **Stay humble and thankful. Give back.**

My Thoughts

Date:

"Success isn't about how much money you make. It's about the difference you make in peoples lives"

~Michelle Obama

CHAPTER 6
LIFE IN GENERAL:

Basic Survival Tips

IDEAS 49-51

49 Keep Calm

There is always a 50% chance that things will always turn out differently as planned. And when faced with such, you must always tackle the situation with much finesse as you can gather. Take a minute to breath, analyze what is happening and then make a decision. This will get you further in life and business. **What situation have you finessed lately?**

50 Face The Challenge

We all face adversity. There is no point trying to avoid it. Challenges are like bullies. Once you stand up to it, it has no choice but to shift its energy and bow in defeat or find someone else to bully. Whatever is at hand and no matter how troublesome it is, facing up to it is often the only way to get it over with. **Success is right over the hill of hard.**

51 Stay Strong

Giving up is easy. Stay strong and stand firm. **You Got This!**

My
Thoughts   Date:

"Fight for the things that you care about, but do it in a way that will lead others to join you"

~Ruth Bader Ginsburg

CHAPTER 7
RELATIONSHIPS:

How To Make Them Last

IDEAS 52-64

Business Relationships: Partners and Clients/Customers

52 Draw The Line

The wrong kind of attachment often destroys the best working relationships. And that is why it is always best to define boundaries from the very beginning. It will not only keep things in check but will also prevent damage control. **It's not personal.**

53 Be Legal

Never mix business with pleasure. To make a business relationship work, partners must always seek the services of a lawyer and an accountant. Not only will they protect the company from failing but will also prevent internal disputes. It truly comes down to what is in black and white. **It's just smart business.**

54 Do Not Be Ignorant

Learn the business. Know what you are getting in to. Know what is expected of you. **Do your due diligence.**

55 Gain The Trust Of Your Customers

Businesses can only thrive if companies develop a trusting relationship with their clients and customers. You are at the helm of this ship. So, start building trust by delivering what you promised. **They will appreciate you more.**

56 Get Feedback

Know what your customer/client needs are. The best way is to ask. Feedback is essential to your business's growth. **Have you asked the question?**

57 Be Ready To Compromise

You should never compromise the integrity of the business, but be open to negotiations. Maintaining a great relationship could prove more profitable in the long run. **It's about the bottom line, but it's not only about the bottom line.**

Personal Relationships: Family, Friendship and Intimate

58 Be Committed

All kinds of relationship need commitment because without it, a relationship will surely fail. May it be for work, in school or the family business, individuals should obligate themselves to perform their side of the bargain. **Who are you down for?**

59 Communication Is Key

If you really want your partnership to work, then master the art of talking and listening. It is the single most powerful secret to every other kind of relationship that exists. **What did you hear them say?**

60 Know When To Reciprocate

Many personal relationships fail because partners do not know how to respond properly. There are no hard or fast rules to developing or nurturing a relationship, you should be willing to let go and let God. **Give what you want to receive.**

61 Be Creative

All relationships go through cycles. It's not going to always be excitement, but keep in mind that boring can lead to disinterest. Challenge yourself and look for ways to spark curiosity or inject life into the relationship. Families need to go on a vacation, friends need to catch up and couples should be spontaneous. **What can you do to keep the creativity flowing?**

62 BE YOURSELF

We all have met representatives and presented our representatives, right? Regardless of how well behaved you pretend you are the real you will eventually show up. How about sooner than later? We don't have time to waste. Let's get to know each other for who we truly are. That way we all have a fair chance to decide if we want to move forward. **Will the real you please stand up?**

63 SAY I'M SORRY

The ego will want you to be right, but it is okay to admit when you are wrong. Saying I am sorry can put a quick end to what the ego will drag out. Allow yourself a minute to breath, but when you are wrong be the bigger person. The sooner the better. **When was the last time you said I'm sorry?**

64 Show Some Love

Sometimes it is not enough that you belong to a family. Children often long for their parents to hug them or pat them on the shoulder. Friends want more than having a good time. A call just to check up on them would be nice. Your significant other may enjoy simply holding hands or a kiss on the forehead. It is important to learn a person's love language. What is the thing that brings them joy or makes them smile? **A simple gesture of love will go a long way.**

My Thoughts

Date:

"You don't need someone to complete you. You only need someone to accept you completely"

~Unknown

CHAPTER 8
SHIT HAPPENS:

How To Win With Everyday Agonies

PRINCIPLES 65-71

65 That Day of the Week

So many people hate when that day of the week rolls around. It's like a thorn in their side, but the funny thing is it happens EVERY WEEK. So, why do you waste energy hating it so much? Learn to embrace it. I created the **#TGIM, The Grace Includes Monday**. Every day that we are blessed to wake up, use our limbs, have a job to go to or a business to run, we are blessed and should be grateful because unfortunately over the weekend someone did not make it to see that next Monday. So, **be happy that you have been given the grace to make Monday great for you and your family.**

66 BE PATIENT

If there is traffic, no sense in getting angry just sit back and wait it out. If your ride is running late, just wait a bit and it will come eventually. These are examples of daily nuisances that people get caught up with, but instead of hating every minute of it, why not just extend your patience a little longer and things will eventually fall in place. **What was the last situation you knew you could have been more patient with?**

67 INSIDE YOUR HEAD

That voice inside your head just won't shut up sometimes. It just chatters away. And most of the time it is negative chatter. Learn to recognize when it is going off into a tangent then shift its focus on to something positive. My mother would say the Lord's Prayer. **What is your positive go to mantra?**

68 Empty Promises

Sometimes you may just end up with people who cannot get the meaning of doing what they say they will do and you get nothing but "sorry" or "I'll do better next time." This is really exasperating especially when you are the one quick to answer someone's need. So, instead of getting angry, understand that everyone will not respond how you would and you should not expect them too. Also, you have the option of not dealing with that person or limiting your graciousness with that person. **The choice is yours.**

69 Horrible Date

When all you wanted was to enjoy a perfect date night and the person turns out not to be so perfect. Again, you have options. You can be honest and just end the date early, you can push through it and stay and eat up anyway or you can excuse yourself to the restroom and call an uber to get you the hell out of there. **How did you handle your last not so perfect date?**

70 Age Ain't Nothing But A Number

We are all going to get there. Getting older is just part of the circle of life so stop tripping on your age. Learn to grow older gracefully and know you are not the first or last person age will happen to. **When they ask how old you are, say it loud and proud.**

71 Wanting to Do More

We all get to a place in our life where we feel the need to do more, but are unsure how or what to do. The rewards of being able to give back to the community can be more therapeutic than you think. You do not have to make your own foundation or create your own nonprofit. Choose a cause to support. Offering your time and talents pro bono could be the way to go. You never know who you will meet or what you will learn and most important the lives you will touch. **What cause is close to your heart?**

My Thoughts

Date:

"Shit Happens. That is the quote. That's it, that's all."

~Sinita Wells

CHAPTER 9
BEATING THE ODDS:
When Things Do Not Go As Expected

PRINCIPLES 72-75

72 Having Expectations

One of the biggest problems we put on ourselves is having expectations. We expect people to do as we do, act as we believe they should, respond how we think they should respond, be who we expect them to be. And the truth of the matter is, it is their life and their only obligation is to live it how they see fit. No one owes no one anything. Whatever decisions people make for themselves they must deal with whatever the consequences are, good and/or bad. Stop getting caught up in YOUR idea of who or what someone should be or do. You can deal with who they are or not. When it's time for them to answer to their God, trust me YOU will not be asked your opinion. **#realtalk**

7.3 Talk To Someone About It

It may take a while but talking to someone about pain is more important than you might think. Nurturing the angst, hurt and pain can sometimes be more than you can handle alone. So, before you breakdown, **seek the help of someone you trust** who can listen to your every word and offer sound advice.

7.4 Quiet Time

Find a place of solitude and pray or meditate for about 10-15 minutes a day. It is often a great way to comfort yourself. Then turn your smart tv to YouTube and **find a beautiful jazz music video** and let it play in the background. It's so soothing.

7.5 Be Ready To Forgive

When there is someone to blame, it is often difficult to move on from it. Being able to forgive is not about them, but more about your wellbeing. Moving on is not easy, but necessary for the preservation of self. Forgiveness is not about forgetting. It's about setting yourself free, mind, body and soul. **Find your peace.**

My Thoughts

Date:

"Don't expect more from others than you're willing to expect from yourself"

~Sinita Wells

CHAPTER 10
BEATING THE ODDS:

When Broken Relationships Do Not Go As Expected

PRINCIPLES 76-80

76 It's Not A Unique Situation

People get their hearts broken all the time. As difficult as it may seem, relationships end and it may not be the ending that you hoped for, but it is what it is. Get out of your head and ego. Take some time to feel the hurt and regroup. Take this as an opportunity to learn more about you. Also, know that you are not alone and as the late great Maya Angelou said, **"This Too Shall Pass"**.

77 Getting Closure

Closure does not always come in the form of the other person saying I'm sorry. If they do, great, but if not, you must be willing to find closure in your own understanding. Maybe that is professional help or simply finding it in your heart to forgive. Either way you must find a way to move on. **How did you find closure?**

78 Mend It

Not all broken relationships are meant to end and if you know or if you are certain that you are simply having a rough patch then find a way to work on it and work it out. Do not simply let it go because it seems to be the easy route. My mother says she never walks away from a relationship until she feels like she has done ALL that is within her power to make it better. **Have you done ALL that you can do?**

79 Lower Your Pride

Love is never often without pride and sometimes, it is the ego that ruins a good relationship. When such thing happens, make sure you know when to raise a white flag. Be the first one to apologize. **It's okay to not always be right.**

80 Hang Out With New People

Meeting new people or hanging out with friends is the quickest way to move on from a dysfunctional relationship. Not that you are so callous about it, but sometimes, when things have come to a full stop there is simply no sense of waiting around. Find ways to occupy your mind. **Time heals or at least make the pain more bearable.**

My Thoughts

Date:

"The way I see it, If you want the rainbow, you gotta put up with the rain"

~Dolly Parton

CHAPTER 11
GUILTY AS CHARGED:

When The Problem Is You

PRINCIPLES 81-85

81 (Wo) Man in the Mirror

Self-inventory is one of the hardest things for a person to do. To be able to look in the mirror and accept responsibility for your part in the situation is big. It is the right and best thing you can do for all involved. The sooner you can accept responsibility, the sooner the healing can begin. None of us are perfect. We are human-beings that do human things. **What do you need to take responsibility for?**

82 Honesty is the Best Policy

It is natural for people at fault to fabricate the truth to side with their version of the story. It is a common reaction, but again, it only delays the true reality which only delays the healing process. **The truth will set you free.**

83 Give In To An Intervention

Earlier we talked about getting help. Allow those that love you to help you or be open to seeking professional help. Again, this may not be as easy as it sounds, but you must recognize when people are only trying to help you be better. **You may not have all the answers and that's alright.**

84 Do Not Lose Hope

Hope is not a bad thing to hold onto. Hoping for a better ending is not a crime. Hope could be the very thing to keep you motivated. Don't ever lose hope. **Keep hope alive.**

85 Let The Past Be The Past

There is no way to change what has already happened. You can't take it back. The only goal should be to move forward. Learn from what the past was there to teach you and do better next time. No sense in holding yourself hostage to the past. **Make peace with it and start fresh.**

My Notes

Date:

"Self-Inventory is not easy, but it's absolutely necessary"

~Sinita Wells

CHAPTER 12
REGAINING YOUR STRENGTH:

In Life, Love and Everything Else

PRINCIPLES 86-96

86 Find New Meaning

This may sound absurd especially when you have hit rock bottom, but it may just be what needed to happen. Just because it did not turn out the way you thought it should have does not mean that was not how it was supposed to happen. Look at it through different eyes or set your sites on an entirely different view. **When one door closes, go through a window.**

87 Redefine Your Goals

Failure does not have to mean you failed. It could mean that adventure was not for you. When starting anew, it may be best to change everything completely. Attempt new goals differently from how you attempted before. **Hit the reset button.**

88 Rehabilitate Your Mind And Body

Go to therapy, go to the gym, go for a swim, if you have to, but you definitely need to work on your muscles and brain activity to get things started again. A healthy you make for a better you. **Love You FIRST.**

89 Seek Spiritual Advice

Religion or no religion, following and listening to a higher being will lead you to a better path. At times when everything seems so lost, the only thing that can fill in the void are words from your spiritual source. Listen closely, **Amen.**

90 Take Up A New Hobby

Try getting out of your comfort zone and learn a new sport or activity. Team up with a new set of friends that like to do different things. You will soon realize that tweaking your hobbies can be enough to re-invent your persona. **Be open to new things.**

91 Retail Therapy

Nothing feels better than a good shopping spree (if you can afford it). Having a new look can surely make you feel good. **So, treat yourself and don't feel guilty about it.**

92 Unplug

Taking a break from social media can be the key to your rejuvenation. If you are a person in business, your business can still run with automation systems in place while you're on the beach far away from wi-fi. **Ahhh, an umbrella in my drink and sand between my toes. YES!**

93 Stroke The Brush

You need not emulate Picasso when you decide to do some painting but just do it to see how you react with the play of colors. Colors often allow people to remember a happier thought, which could be enough to revive a lost soul. Add a glass of wine and soft music to boot. **Set the mood.**

94 Learn To Say No

People can be insanely polite at times, too polite that they say yes when they really want to say a resounding no. This is the most common way of being taken advantage of and it just does not fit well with re-inventing yourself. **One of us will be unhappy and it won't be me.**

95 Do Something Radical

Get a tattoo, dye your hair or take a solo trip. Consider it a big hurrah as part of the rebuilding **YOU process.**

96 Reclaim Your Mind

Do not spend another minute on people, places and/or things that do not serve you. Things that are meaningless should not be given the opportunity to operate inside your brain. You are working to build an empire. So, seeds need to be planned in your mind that generate new ideas and action plans that bring your hopes, dreams and wishes closer to fruition. It is harvest time. **I am reclaiming my mind.**

My thoughts

Date:

"Don't be a Lady.
Be a Legend"

~Stevie Nicks

CHAPTER 13
END OF THE ROAD:

Zoning In On What You Want

PRINCIPLES 97-102

97 TAKE CONTROL OF YOUR LIFE

Enough with all the what-ifs and what not and simply take over your ideals and make them real. Dreams only become reality when you wake up and take action. Rome was not built in a day, but it was built. **You are the captain of this ship.**

98 DISCIPLINE YOURSELF

If you do not want to be fat, then watch what you eat. If you want a higher salary, then work on impressing the boss and if you want to start anew, better start acting on it. Become whatever it is you want to be. **Seeing is believing.**

99 Be Responsible

You cannot blame it all on the economy, supervisors or colleagues. Make up for what you lack and double your efforts. If you want to create a brighter future for yourself, grab this life by the fucking balls and **GO FOR IT!**

100 Accept Your Self

You may never ever get to succeed in life if you keep beating yourself down. Sometimes, you must simply accept who you are and work on a better you. **There is so much more to learn.**

101 You Are Enough

You must accept that you are not perfect and that is okay. You were created just the way you were supposed to be. We can learn new things, change how we look, but the blueprint to who you are is enough. It is a realization that can change the way you look at life and love yourself. **Who loves you baby?**

102 What Is Stopping You?

You can have it all. You just need to decide what all is for you and go after it. Your all is not my all and vice versa. This world is yours. You must learn to be bold enough, conquer your fears, take life by the horns, believe greater, dream bigger and go get that shit. **YOU are your only hold up. #PERIOD!**

My Thoughts

Date:

"If you can dance and be free and not be embarrassed, you can rule the world"

~Amy Poehler

CHAPTER 14
TOP 8 VIRTUES

To Enjoy A More Prosperous Life

1 Faith

There must be something greater than yourself that you believe in. The world evolves daily, the seasons change yearly, babies are created, the body knows how to heal itself so there must be something BIGGER than what we can see. Keeping the faith allows you to trust that everything will find a way to work itself out. **Got to have Faith.**

2 Grace

Individuals should not struggle to adapt to a life filled with grace. Despite all the heartaches and pains, the ups and downs in life, there is an essence of grace that we are all granted. When you did not think that you would make it through it was by grace that you are still here. **Count your blessings.**

3 Love

Love make the world a better place. It is truly the purest of all emotions and exactly what you need to make you better. And because of that, **"All you need is love."**

4 Mercy

Life gets tough. It gets rough and it may seem like there is no way out, but we are all granted mercy. We have done or said things we are not proud of, but we are all granted mercy. For that alone, you owe it to this life to give it everything you got. **Mercy is a saving grace.**

5 Sensitivity

Being connected emotionally is an awesome asset. Knowing how to or when to react to one's need show that you know what it means to be human. We are all part of the human experience and that sometimes require us to be more sensitive to one another. **We may not have walked in their shoes, but we can be sensitive to their journey.**

6 Wonder

To be continuously amazed by things is crucial as it revitalizes the human spirit despite failing circumstances. Being amazed by the biggest of things as well as the smallest of lives little wonders is simply beautiful. **Stay curious**.

7 Service

You are not a lone ranger in this world. If you are fortunate enough to have then you will be blessed when you give. The ability of helping others is a very powerful tool in satisfying the inner self. It can be a small act of kindness that can change someone's entire life direction. **Sharing is Caring.**

8 Knowledge

You don't have to know it all, but know what matters. Knowing what to do, how to act, when to respond and how to do it are important things to own in times of joy and pain. Being able to process an idea has been the only thing that has separated man from the other creatures. Constantly sharpen your intellect by feeding your mind with ideas, thoughts and information. **A mind is a terrible thing to waste so stop doing it.**

vir·tue |
\ ˈvər-(ˌ)chü \
noun
Definition of virtue

1a: conformity to a standard of right : MORALITY

b: a particular moral excellence

~Merriam Webster

Your Biggest Take Aways

from this book

My Thoughts

Date:

My Thoughts

Date:

My Thoughts

Date:

CONCLUSION

Success can be defined in so many different ways. In fact, your definition of victory may be different from your mother's definition, but it serves the same purpose, for you to have a better life.

No matter how mind-boggling life can be, it remains to be a gift that's meant to be enjoyed. Life satisfaction is the ultimate goal. You want to excel in your chosen profession, live happily with your chosen person, raise your family and grow old gracefully. Satisfied that you have done all the things your heart desired and leaving no rocks unturned.

The biggest catch in life is taking the lessons, experiences, moments and memories to live your true authentic self. The soul, the body and the mind can only be accomplished by your own efforts.

Wishing this book to be a keepsake as a reminder of the many principles, ideas and virtues you can use to guide your life. And most of them do not come with a hefty price tag either.

ABOUT THE AUTHOR

Sinita Wells is a confidence mindset coach, content creator and self-published author. Her debut book, I Am A Woman First, The Essentials to Nurturing, Inspiring and Loving You First, empowers women to embrace SELF FIRST by unapologetically putting themselves at the top of their to-do-list.

With her no sugar-coated coaching style and over 20 years of media experience, Sinita's strategies promotes the importance of personal development to fuel business growth through video content formulas and storytelling.

As a believer that the business is only as strong as the woman, Sinita's strategies provide women in business the right steps to build a solid brand foundation for authoritative positioning and profitability in the online space with an unparalleled level of confidence, authenticity, and success.

Are you ready for your Next Level? Schedule time to chat with her and *follow* her in these social media streets to get your whole life.

FOLLOW ME IN THESE INTERNET STREETS

- @sinitawellsdotcom
- @sinitawellsdotcom
- @sinitawellsdotcom
- @sinitawellsdotcom
- @sinitawells
- @sinitawells

SCAN ME!
WWW.SINITAWELLS.COM

www.sinitawells.com

Email: bookings@sinitawells.com

Made in the USA
Columbia, SC
09 July 2022